Books by Stephen J. Lyons

Landscape of the Heart
A View from the Inland Northwest
The 1000-Year Flood
Going Driftless

West of East

essays by

Stephen J. Lyons

Finishing Line Press
Georgetown, Kentucky

West of East

ACKNOWLEDGMENTS

Atticus Review: Boots
The Common: Miguel (as "Hops")
Slag Glass City: Frank
The Sun: Killing Time
Hope Magazine: Standing at the Edge

Publisher: Leah Huete de Maines
Editor: Christen Kincaid
Cover Art: Stephen J. Lyons
Author Photo: Stephen J. Lyons
Cover Design: Elizabeth Maines McCleavy

Printed in the USA on acid-free paper.
Order online: www.finishinglinepress.com
             also available on amazon.com

Author inquiries and mail orders:
Finishing Line Press
P. O. Box 1626
Georgetown, Kentucky 40324
U. S. A.

Table of Contents

for Jan

Boots

Boots taught me how to drink. She lived across the hall from me in a boarding house in southwestern Colorado: three two-room, furnished apartments above the elderly landlord, Mr. Fowler, who charged eighty bucks a month; common bathroom with a claw-foot tub down the hall; and a shared phone at the foot of the stairs. No one bothered to lock their doors.

I was seventeen and on my own for the first time. I worked the fry cook swing shift at the Western Steakhouse with a Chinese-American menu. I took care of the American side of the grill. On the other side Chinese cooks hovered over two giant sizzling woks. Woodrow Wilson Wong was an exacting boss who spoke perfect English when he caught me loafing. "Get to work now! Get to work now!" He said it twice like a mantra and emphasized it with an exacting poke in the ribs. However, when I complained to him about the hours he was cheating me on my paycheck, he lapsed into Mandarin indicating that he did not understand. When I cut my pinkie to the bone on a meat slicer the Chinese cooks stopped the bleeding with raw sage. Afterwards, I sat on the steps outside trying not to look at my finger and pass out until Wong found me, poked me in the ribs and said, "Get to work now! Get to work now!" It was 1974. I made one dollar and sixty cents an hour plus one free meal a shift.

Boots was short with a bleached blonde beehive and a curvaceous figure in decline. She was older, more experienced, and entertained a lot of visitors, mostly men. I could hear their cowboy boots hammer up and down the stairs at all hours and smell their cigarette smoke through the thin walls. Some nights I would wake up to the clink of glasses, shouts, and laughter, then the rhythmic bounce of bedsprings.

The other resident in the boarding house was Jane, on whom I had a crush. She was a student at the local university and drove a Volvo sedan with Illinois plates. Some evenings Jane would invite me over for herbal tea. She wore a thin, revealing nightgown on those nights, but nothing ever came of it. I often thought of her bathing in our common bathtub. When she moved to Albuquerque I typed up a smeary, typo-laden letter in the public library, quoting Steinbeck from "Grapes of Wrath." I can't remember the exact passage but it was something about wanting an honest life and lying down in a field with a woman. When Jane did not reply I hitchhiked down to New Mexico unannounced, where she fed me tacos, put me up for one awkward, celibate night, and in the early morning dropped me off at a freeway on-ramp during a snowstorm.

Boot's door was usually open in the daytime. She dressed in jeans and a western-style shirt. She would sit on her foldout couch, smoking and drinking, looking down at the street from her window and listening on the radio to a talk station out of Denver.

When I passed her apartment on the way to the john she would call out to me and ask if I wanted a drink. The first few times I turned her down thinking that if I was seen with her it might hurt my chances with Jane. But the day I returned bedraggled and deflated from Albuquerque I said, sure, why not? She mixed up a pitcher of gin and tonic on top of her dresser. Up to this point I had only imbibed 3.2 beer. I took right to the juniper taste of gin and, after the second or third glass, I told Boots my sad story of rejection and humiliation in the Land of the Enchantment. She was an attentive listener, nodding her head in sympathy, even putting her arm around me and rocking me gently when I teared up. She smelled of soap and cigarettes, and I began to give in to the exhaustion of the trip. I also realized that I was quite drunk. I excused myself and stumbled back to my room where I slept for twelve hours.

Sometime during the night I vaguely recognized Boots entering my room and opening drawers and cabinets and going through the pockets of my Levis. It seemed like a dream and the gin had taken away most of my vigilance and all my resistance. On her way out she pulled the covers up around my shoulders and kissed my cheek, purring, "You *are* a poor boy, aren't you?"

Since my shift at the Western didn't begin until three in the afternoon I fell into a routine of having drinks with Boots beforehand. I tried to pace myself but I began to crave those gin and tonics, and my work on the grill began to get sloppy. (It was around this time that I cut my pinkie.) I would fall out of rhythm with the orders, cook the fries before making the burger, and start the toast before cracking the eggs to make the omelets, those sorts of rookie mistakes. Wong noticed, too, and gave me two weeks to shape up.

Except for occasional trips to Wagon Wheel Liquors for supplies, Boots rarely left the house. Despite all our afternoons together I never learned why she was called Boots. I only knew the sketchiest outline of her life: she was the daughter of a geologist and grew up in mining camps in Montana and Nevada. Her mother suffered from depression and alcoholism. Boots had a brief marriage to a gambler named Lonny, worked as a showgirl in Reno at one of the minor casinos, and had a grown daughter named Lily, who lived in Haight-Ashbury with a hippie healer. They were not on speaking terms. I never knew how she supported herself, but I began to suspect it had something to do with those gentlemen callers.

The day I was fired I had been drinking with Boots since mid morning. Boots had a fresh shiner on her left eye. I asked what had happened. She sighed, exhaled a perfect smoke ring, and said there had been a little misunderstanding. She and a fellow had gone out to the Strater Hotel for a nightcap and run into the guy's wife, who been searching every bar in town for her husband. She pulled Boots right off the bar stool, slugged her with a fist that featured a couple of nice fat Zuni inlaid rings. In her other hand she carried a cast iron skillet, about the right size for two eggs over easy. She then dragged her husband out of the bar by his hair. As was the custom around there, no one bothered to call the police.

"How was I supposed to know he was married? Guys never wear rings," Boots explained.

She seemed nervous and kept looking out the window as if expecting more visits from angry spouses.

"I gotta get out of here. Maybe head down to Flagstaff."

"What about Reno?" I asked.

"Oh, no," Boots said. "I can never go back there."

Boots was mixing progressively stronger drinks and by noon I was well past sober. I knew I couldn't face Wong and another shift of slinging fried egg sandwiches and patty melts so I simply didn't go in. The phone downstairs rang at 3:15, then again every fifteen minutes for an hour, but I didn't answer. I wasn't too worried. Rent was due the next day, but I'd been paid the night before and I had $300 stashed in a teapot, so I could afford to coast for a couple of months. Maybe I'd take another trip down to Albuquerque or take a backpacking trip into the lake country above Silverton. Boots kept filling my glass until the spinning began.

When I woke up it was early afternoon of the next day. I could barely stand upright. I tried to recall how I had managed to undress and get into bed but all I could remember was Boots insisting that I try a double. I walked into my tiny kitchen and noticed that the lid of the teapot was off center. The cash was gone, of course. I rushed across the hall but Boots' apartment was vacant, the bed made up, the hangers in the closet shoved to one side, and the dresser drawers empty. There was not even one bit of trash anywhere in the rooms. It was if she had never existed. I went back to my apartment, looked in the mirror, and noticed that I had a lipstick kiss on my right cheek.

I found Mr. Fowler on the front porch reading the *Durango Herald*. I sat down next to him and told him the rent would be late. Without looking up he said, "A Woodrow Wong called. He said you're fired." As we sat there a pickup truck with Arizona plates pulled up. A young Navajo man about my age with two waist-length black braids jumped out of the passenger side. He walked right up to Mr. Fowler, and without a word handed him an envelope and left. Mr. Fowler opened it and I could see it was full of ten- and twenty-dollar bills. Mr. Fowler laughed and slapped his thigh.

"I loaned this kid $500 more than a year ago. Thought I'd never see it again and here he shows up unannounced and pays me back. You never know what's going to happen, do you?"

Miguel

When we were young and poor, they handed us dull machetes. At first light, in the back of half-ton grain trucks, we rode past the peppermint fields and pear orchards of southern Oregon. We were strangers thrown together like dogs in a kennel. Some of us smoked quietly or blew the steam off the tops of take-out coffee containers. Others sipped whiskey from dented flasks or spit tobacco into plastic bottles. In ratty plaid shirts, torn dungarees, and inadequate footwear we looked the part of migrant workers. We would work twelve hours with a half-hour break at lunch that felt like no break at all. At the end of our shift we were older, more broken and still in debt.

Hops fields are jungles of rope-like vines climbing trellises to a height of more than ten feet. The narcotic plant did two things to me—it made me sleepy and it ate through my clothing. There was no formal training, but it was understood that I was to be hoisted up in a bucket attached to a tractor to cut the thick vines at the top of the plant. The long clump would fall into a trailing truck. When we reached the end of the row it was also understood that I would sharpen my machete with a whetstone, something I had never done before. Neither the tractor nor the truck would ever stop moving.

The combination of machetes and men—many of whom were moonlighting and had not slept for days—was fraught with danger. By mid-morning on the first day of harvest three men were sent to the ER with bad cuts, and two guys named Buzzard and Rock were sent packing after a fistfight. The last I saw of them they were leaving the field in the back of a truck while pounding each other in the face. I learned later that they were first cousins.

Another guy, who kept a moleskin notebook in his back pocket, wore a checkered *kaffiyeh* head scarf around his neck and a Che Guevara T-shirt, made a scene and told the foreman he had bad karma. Che was fired on the spot. Later I heard he left a long note—more of a manifesto—about workers' rights and the rising power of the proletariat on the windshield of the foreman's truck.

The foreman with the bad karma, Miguel, wore a cap advertising the herbicide paraquat. Anger was his overriding emotion. Rage trailed not far behind. When he loaded us in the trucks at dawn he said, "You know, when I first come to this country you *putos* disrespected me and my family. I do not forget such things." He spit something thick and yellowish in our direction and slammed the tailgate.

I tried as hard as I could to stay out of the way of Miguel but there is no place to hide when you are riding high above everyone else in a bucket. I felt like I was atop an elephant. Miguel sensed my fear and soon turned his vindictive wrath toward me. I was made an example of how not to do things: How not to sharpen the machete. How not to cut the vines. How not to keep up.

As I hacked away, my arms screaming in pain, I contemplated my limited options. I could quit, but I was a broke twenty-year-old with no prospects, squatting in a camper trailer along the Rogue River on land belonging to a family of paranoid biker pot growers. The place was infested with timber rattlers basking on rocks in front of the trailer during the day. I needed this miserable job.

When lunch finally arrived I barely had the energy to eat a soggy cheese sandwich and an apple. I watched as Miguel's family joined him. His wife had a thick waist and a long braid of dark hair. She laid out plastic plates filled with tamales and roasted corn on a blanket as three thin giggly girls in summer dresses twirled around their father. Miguel could not stop smiling as he hugged and tickled them. He looked over at me and nodded as if to say, see, *puto*, you could not defeat me. I have everything I need. You have nothing. I smiled back not quite understanding that he was right.

Frank

Years ago I lived in Tucson's Skid Row. That is where I met Frank. At the time I drove an ice cream truck for a company called Miss Sharon's. My boss cashed me out each night with a loaded .357 magnum resting on his desk between us so there would be no arguments when he shortchanged me. There were none. Frank used to hang out at the shuffleboard courts, just down the street from the plasma donor center. Despite our age difference, we took to each other right way. Over time, we told each other our stories. I was an inexperienced hippie with a guitar and a notebook, and a dream of being the next Dylan, Jack Kerouac, or Jack London. Frank? His ambitions were quite different. Unlike me, he had lived a long, tough life.

After each conversation I would hurry back to my apartment and jot down his words as best as I could remember in a small, cloth notebook with the word "Record" stamped in gold type on the cover. At the time, it felt like the most important thing in the world to be doing. As if I might just be a writer after all.

Anyway, I hope Frank forgives me if the following is not a word-for-word recollection of our talks, and if I took a few authorial liberties in the retelling. Somehow, I bet he'd be okay with it.

"In 1940 I was shipped down here by bus from the state hospital in Medical Lake, Washington. Doctors determined from some tests involving electricity that I was officially *normal*, or at least not any kind of threat to anyone except myself and that never counted for shit. So they set me free, to roam with twenty-six bucks, a comb, leather hiking boots, a one-way ticket to Arizona, and thirteen bottles of blue and green pills—someone's bright idea to stop these voices I've been hearing. But I threw all the pills away in Boise just after I started to see two of everything. Did not like that. Seeing one of anything is plenty. I'm officially called *disabled*, "not suitable for employment." That's what it says right here on these papers I keep in my socks. What them papers don't say is that I can walk farther than anyone, that I love the desert at night more than anything else and that I seen a lot of things in this certifiably crazy world. Hey, I'm not the only one. Tucson is a dumping ground for us homeless and so-called bums. We're like some lost tribe of wrinkly men, hanging out in what's left of downtown, bumming dimes off heat-seeking tourists from Iowa who flock down here in the winter to warm up and have themselves a Native American-Southwest-Kokopelli-cultural experience. I've never seen unhappier people in my eighty years. Unlike that bunch—and the rest of the world—we homeless respect each other's privacy and space. We say exactly what we think. No filters. Tourists don't much like that but truth ain't for the faint of heart. Sure, some of us drink ourselves into a white heat. I confess I'm no angel on that score. And the younger ones out here are dangerous. They'll open up your gut with a rusty blade for a few quarters. Drugs make 'em do it—all that crack business with the pipes and needles—and I don't mess with drugs. No sir. This here life is strange enough as it is without throwing drugs into the mix. Cops ain't much better either. Again, it's those itchy younger ones who don't respect anything older than yesterday.

As for me? I ride the Sun-Trans bus every day of the year. Call it my day job. The drivers mostly leave me alone because I don't talk out loud, don't stink, and I don't panhandle anybody. And unlike most folks, I know where I'm headed. I take the Number 8 right out of Ronstadt Transfer Station down Broadway to Alvernon where I switch to the 14, which goes east to the last stop at the Botanical Gardens. Ever been there? Then I walk straight into the desert. No one can out walk yours truly. I'm like a tank. I never stumble, and I can see at night like a tomcat. I've been as far east as the Chiricahua Mountains, west all the way to Quintobaquito, south into Mexico to Los Tajitos. I stay away from the north, up by Phoenix and Scottsdale. Too many voices up there. I know every seam and crease of Sabino Canyon, even drank with the WPA bridge builders camped out there in the 40s when there were still trout in the creek and not those useless sunfish.

Look, I ain't stupid. I listen and the desert's been telling me her secrets. I've taught myself to identify all the cacti and cholla. And I can tell the exact day, precisely, more or less, because things are changing fast down here, when the ocotillo blooms; how long it takes a saguaro to grow its first elbow; how many thorns there are on each ear of a prickly pear; what direction a rattler coils; why we need bats. And I learned some other things, too, all of 'em probably not too useful to anyone around here from what I can tell. I know where the desert tortoises live, but I'll never tell anyone. I've seen ocelots, ring tails, wolves that ain't supposed to be here, coral snakes as lit up as Christmas lights, and one fat Mexican grizzly with the face as big as an eighteen-wheeler's hubcap. I've even spotted jaguar tracks. Don't ask me where. These lips are sealed. And I've seen the families, women and children mostly, crossing the desert from Mexico, always running, always looking over their shoulders like scared jackrabbits, throwing themselves right into the thorn bushes to avoid the border patrol whose vision is even better than mine. Hey, those families are alright by me, and I give 'em what I can: water, oranges, bus tokens, cigarettes, some of my government money, though it ain't never enough.

But, look, things are dying out there, out beyond the golf courses, the condos, the super malls that won't let the likes of me inside, past all of them new lawns with their goddamned sprinklers that run full blast in the middle of the day, and them houses that remind me of tombs. Dying, every last bit of it. White-barked sycamores, live oaks, cottonwoods, velvet ash. All of 'em retreating back down the hills, crowding into the last slips of creek, spring, and shade. Even the saguaros. Why the hell should anyone believe me? I'm just an old bum with rotten teeth that hears voices. But every day them voices get louder. It's kinda like a million mountain lions screaming at the same time. 'Cept it's the desert screaming. Know how they make the desert scream? They use these three-story-sized earth movers with chains to drag out the paloverde and the mesquite, the tortoises and the Gilas, hedgehog cactus, anything and everything that gets caught in the teeth of them machines,

And they work at night when they figure no one's around. But I see 'em alright, yeah I see 'em, chewing up the desert, pissing on everything, throwing them damn beer cans in the brush, stomping on the lizards and scorpions, generally making a holy mess of things. Everyone's in on it. It's one big land and plant grab. They dig up the jumping chollas, cow skulls, rocks, Indian drawings, and ship 'em off to them health spas in Sedona or Santa Fe. Then the javelinas and lions and anything that can outrun the machines head further south toward Nogales, and Heaven help 'em down there.

Me? I've run out of places to run to. Besides, I want to be right here, in

Tucson with my buddies, when this city gets the dry heaves, when the water runs out, when the sprinklers quit hissing, when the swimming pools evaporate, when the entire stinking mess comes crashing to a goddamn halt, pardon my French. Now some years back I heard people on the buses talk about saving water, pulling up the Kentucky bluegrass and letting the desert come back. But now no one mentions water. A thousand people a month are moving down here, mostly lawn lovers from Canada and Ohio. They don't care about water. They ain't listening. They don't hear nothing 'cause they're too busy talking. But I'm doing everything I can to save the desert. I don't leave the tap on anymore when I wash up at the Greyhound station. When I see people hosing down their sidewalks I give 'em the evil eye. I haven't flushed a toilet in ten years. See, I pay attention to my friends—the plants and animals. They tell me to lie low during the day when it's hot, like a lizard does, to shut down my body; to do my walking at night when it's cooler. Last summer the temperature got to 130, and I did just fine.

Now, I still got me some good friends down in the Barrio. Like me, they feel squeezed out by the New Agers, the architects and painters who think the neighborhood is charming—authentic, whatever that means. Hell, they even named it the "Art District." But to us it's our home 'cause it's familiar. It's all we got besides the medicine and each other. On Saturday nights, if I'm not out walking, and the cops are chewing on donuts somewhere, we all get together—the old timers that is—at the shuffleboard courts. We pass a little malt beer around and swap stories about old Tucson, the way it was before the gangs and the crystal meth and the forty-million-dollar Civic Center that cut the heart out of this here city and pushed out from the center of things. This was some sweet city. A hobo's paradise. Lemons, oranges, grapefruits would fall into your hands. You had to be a fool to starve. There were hummingbirds and flickers in every tree and bush. Varieties of birds and flowers you ain't never going to see again. Less cops, more trains. No malls filled with useless plastic junk and them kids with their hats turned the wrong way. And a hell of a lot more water.

Back then the voices were only whispering to me. Lately I don't feel that good myself. I guess me and the desert are on the same time line, health-wise. We're running out of time and energy. Not to mention that H2O business. We can't fight 'em anymore. Too many machines. Who knows how long we'll hold out. I figure I'm about ready to call it quits. Let someone else have this here job. There's only so much change a person can fit into one lifetime and not get their heart hurt. One of these days, and soon, I'm walking out into the sagebrush and I ain't ever coming back. I know just the place, too. Out there to the southeast, past Dos Cabezas, in the Chiricahuas. No voices anywhere around, 'cept the good ones like gray jays, coyotes, owls, red tails. And there's these trees, they call 'em *alligator junipers*, with this funny black bark that looks like its been all burnt to Hell and stitched back together, like an ugly puzzle, like yours truly. Growed to be sixty-feet tall with branches sticking out every which way because the wind makes things interesting up there. I always figured them junipers to be my good luck trees. Like we share some big secret. Anyways, I'm going to lie down under the biggest one I can find in the canyon, look up through those branches with their purple-green berries that stink like skid row gin, close these old sunburnt eyes, and think about how I got here, all them long walks under the stars in the desert. I'll retrace every step I ever took in the last fifty years. I'll sort the whole damn thing out once and for all. And I'm going to remember every plant, animal, and snake, that fat grizzly, too; all my hobo buddies down on Congress Street, who, by the way, ain't looking too sharp themselves, and all them Mexican families that never hurt nobody and just want a chance at something better. By the time I'm found, my bones will be as white as widow's hair. The smart ones will find me first, the coyotes and bobcats. Maybe a little band of javelinas will poke around after that, although I won't have too much they'd be wanting. Then the buzzards and the ants can pick through what's left and scatter these old bones all over southern Arizona and Sonora. I'd be giving something back to this desert, such as it is.

I got no regrets, either. I gave this here life my best shot. Listened to the voices, behaved myself on the buses, didn't waste no water, never harmed even a fly. No sir. I only got one favor to ask. When I'm gone please tell someone about the machines, how they're stealing all the beauty in this world. Tell 'em enough is enough. We already got us enough cars, guns, and televisions, and a million other things to make us all jittery. As it is, the world's running too fast for a person to think about any important stuff like frogs and lizards, stars and river rocks. What we need is some places to walk at night so folks can move around quiet-like and breathe deep, not always get in each other's way. We need less roads and more things we can love that ain't ever gonna change; that the earth movers can't haul away. If you want to know what I'm talking about, go check on those white sycamores down in Sabino Canyon. Sit yourself down next to 'em, and listen. But just remember, bring lots of water. It's getting dry down there, bone dry."

Killing Time

For a time, when the baby was still in diapers, when jobs were scarce all up and down the Pacific Coast, and when the years ahead seemed infinite, I would spend an occasional afternoon in a neighborhood bar in Eureka, California. The bar, which I never frequented during the night, sat next to a Laundromat where, between dollar-draft beers, I would wash, dry, and fold my family's modest collection of Goodwill scraps. The San Francisco Giants aired in variable states of visibility on the bar's color television (this was before cable and satellite). While the bartender replenished free helpings of salty popcorn, I sat on a stool to watch the latest daytime baseball drama, trying unsuccessfully to avoid the reflection of my idleness in the large mirror that sat behind the amber-colored bottles of Jim Beam, Cuervo Gold and Wild Turkey. I wasn't entirely alone. There were the usual older men seen in bars who had been drinking since the morning and would probably be drinking until last call.

Despite my support, the Giants weren't going anywhere in the early 1980s and I guess I wasn't either, sitting in a dark tavern in the middle of the weekday between cycles, drinking beer and watching my life tick away pitch by pitch, inning by inning. I was a prisoner to an oppressive feeling of waiting—waiting to wake up and take hold of my twenty-something life, waiting, I guess, to eventually give in and occupy the world of homeowners and pension holders: positions that, honestly, I wanted nothing to do with and that I routinely mocked. I thought that, at the most, a passion would take root or, at the very least, a lucky break might come my way. But I lacked a real plan. Thinking back, I do believe I wanted to live under the radar like a poet, scribbling breathless prose in my journals and making just enough money to buy a weekly box of grains and cheeses at the Arcata Food Coop. Back in the late 1970s and early 1980s you could live such a life and still hold together a family. The world was more forgiving toward slackers and dreamers.

I was in a state of delusion, of course, not only about the world and my future, but also about the present. For there were many days I didn't write in my journal and I didn't look for ways to better my family's economics. I simply did nothing. I know now, from a distance of forty years, we are given a certain unknown amount of days in our short lives and each one should be handled like a precious, breakable gem. The moments wasted in stupor, meaningless labor or (how to solve this!) in slumber can never be recovered. And I've frittered away my share, always foolishly betting on the redemption of the remaining days yet to come.

My starts and stops at inhabiting a life took me all over northern California, through the awesome groves of threatened redwoods to the soggy coastal bottoms filled with egrets, both great and snowy. In the hills above Petrolia, I spent a week earning a certificate qualifying me to shear sheep. (I had a momentary fantasy of starting my own shearing business, traveling the curvaceous country roads from farm to farm, trimming wool and listening to the stories of rural America.) The instructor, a New Zealander who went by the name Barton, would not tolerate slackers or wise guys. When he wasn't criticizing our clumsy techniques, pointing out the bloody nicks and gouges we inflicted on the poor Merinos, he spun fabulous tales of shearing competitions Down Under, where the wool flew off in record time and where the bars were so wild they had to be hosed down at the end of each night. Like the old joke, Barton came from a place where men were men and the sheep were scared. But, like most physical tasks, I was hopeless at this one, too. My hands oozed lanolin while my confidence sagged when I realized that sheep would not be in my future.

Then it was on to a weeklong non-violent workshop in Eureka for anti-nuke activists. When we were finished with our training we would be sent to central California to protest the imminent construction of the Diablo Canyon Nuclear Power Plant that happened to be sited on the same location as a major earthquake fault. I stood in a line in a stranger's living room with other well-meaning novices while a man poked us hard in our chests and yelled nasty things about our hair, politics, and work habits. Like little Gandhi clones, we were instructed to take the abuse, not to respond in a like manner and, in fact, sit in a lotus position until we were hauled away by the authorities.

But the nonviolence didn't take. What I really wanted to do was punch this guy hard in the kisser so he would stop shouting. I had never felt so much rage before. And this was on the first day! A spaghetti and salad potluck followed the hazing, but I slipped out the backdoor never to return. OK, so I wasn't Gandhi. But just who was I?

I next tried my hand as a tree planter. Although the job was simple— every nine feet dig a hole and insert a tree plug—I was unsuited for the backbreaking labor performed in driving rain on vertical slopes. Each morning at 4:30 a.m., about fifteen of us would board a beat-up van to be dumped off at some distant spot in the slick, coastal hills of clear-cut forests. On the way we would debate politics, discuss books and debate the latest food fetishes.

"I heard that wheat grass juice makes your memory sharper."

"Only if you mix it with equal parts carrot juice."

"I thought it was beet juice and spirulina."

"I don't remember."

Those discussions with other young men in the same stage of career inertia had an enabling effect that was not unlike a narcotic. We were the tribe of the longhaired, bearded, and uninsured, We dressed in colorful natural fibers. Armed with our dog-eared copies of "Be Here Now," "Zen in the Art of Archery," and "Co-Evolution Quarterly," we were searching for a higher meaning beyond the America Dream of accumulation and status. Meanwhile, our more focused peers were getting their MBAs, medical and law degrees, and already gathering capital. They had health insurance, mortgages, and dependable cars. We had wild hair and attitude. Who was more centered? And did we with our ponytails really have more idealism than our peers climbing confidently toward middle class and beyond? At the age of twenty I certainly thought we did.

Tree planting was classic mind-numbing piecework. Experienced planters literally ran up and down the hillsides quickly digging holes and jamming hemlock seedlings into them with one fluid motion. I was more thoughtful in my approach and hampered by a thickening depression brought on by my work environment. The land on which we planted trees was a barren moonscape. Just days before stood a magnificent old growth diverse forest full of birds and bears and owls. The new wasteland was mute except for the rapacious sounds of chainsaws from the next ridge over. I often paused to look over the battlefield (and to straighten my aching back). During those moments, as other planters ran past me with the agility of mountain goats, I could not get over the loss of trees or the scope of environmental destruction. How could these tiny nursery seedlings I was shoving into the soil ever replace a mature forest? I barely made twenty bucks a day. After three weeks I simply ignored the alarm clock one morning. I certainly was not missed.

There were other attempts at economic normalcy: a failed try-out as a milker at a dairy and a five-minute job at a nursing home, where I walked into the day room, took one look around at the traffic jam of elderly residents slumped in wheelchairs, punched the time clock and slipped out. I spent two days working for an angry roofer who never said a word until he fired me, and I clocked three days cutting hops in southern Oregon before I was fired for telling the foreman he had bad karma, which, I assure you, he did. Really bad karma.

I actually made it through two, month-long seasons of daffodil picking, stooped over (once again) in the unceasing coastal drizzle, bundling a dozen yellow stalks at a time with a rubber band and dropping them off at the end of the endless rows. The daffodils were shipped across the country for families to place on their dining room tables to brighten the cloudy days of late winter. As I felt the cold, muddy water seep into my shoes and socks, I told myself that I was helping to alleviate America's winter blues. That seemed to help me get through the long hours. The same young men—and, this time, young women—that planted trees labored alongside me. We were all white kids, drawn to the fields by the freedom of piecework and, I suppose, the romanticism of a migrant life. When the season ended—around the first week of February—some of the pickers collected unemployment, some continued to live off the grid in vans or squat in teepees on public lands, while others moved on to the next seasonal job. But I now suspect that more than a few of my fellow pickers went directly to a college admissions office. Hard work in the rain has a way of converting the most radical holdouts to the warm, dry world of the student.

During my two seasons of cold mud and yellow bulbs, I made friends with a couple. Let's call them Jon and Becky. They lived the life I thought I should be living: moving from state to state like migratory birds, following the crops from south to north, never setting down roots. They were the fastest daffodil pickers and, because they worked as a team and pooled their earnings, they made more money than any of us. Sometimes we would gather after work at their furnished rental in the fog-enshrouded town of Samoa, on Humboldt Bay. Over miso soup, crusty baguettes of tangy sourdough, and soft chunks of havarti, Jon and Becky would spin stories of their itinerant travels: cherry picking in Michigan, peach harvest in the South, and the red delicious apple harvest up in Washington state. They cast their bedrolls on the edges of fields and orchards and in forest service campgrounds. They worked hard, cashed their paychecks, and then hit the road, never leaving a trace. The land is magical, Jon said. It holds all the answers. And, among us, it was understood that the goal of this short life was to live as close to soil, roots, and weather as possible. To unplug from society and to work outdoors. To regularly watch the sunset and the moon rise. To pay attention in a world of sleepwalkers.

The couple seemed holy to me, and I longed to follow them, to be close to them, to learn how to live against the grain, and how to relax with the choice. Somewhere along the way I lost track of them. The addresses they gave me were all general delivery addresses in towns like Canyonville, Oregon, and Marquette, Michigan, and after awhile whatever infrequent letters I sent came back, address unknown. I often wonder how long they held out or if they finally gave in to comfort and security. Did they maintain their independence? How did those years of migrating affect the rest of their lives? Was it the right decision?

Between jobs, I retreated to my neighborhood tavern to kill time and catch up with the dismal Giants. The news was not encouraging. We were all in a slump. The team consistently finished between third and fifth place in the early 1980s and I never could make a decent wage. In 1982, a typical year of underachievement, my odd collection of odd jobs added up to an income of $6,351. Finally, in 1985, I cashed in my migrant chips and began classes at the University of Idaho. Looking back, I want to believe that my attitude hadn't changed and that it was only having the demands of a young family that pushed me to improve my lot. But, truthfully, I could not longer push against the tide of conformity.

I am now three times as old as that twenty-year-old kid who picked daffodils and hops, planted trees, drove tractors, and sat in a dimly-lit bar in California contemplating his next move. My life is settled. My daughter is married to a great man and I am remarried to a wonderful woman. I have work that engages me. I know my limitations professionally and personally. I have a dependable car and health insurance. My modest nest egg grows and there is a fifty-fifty chance I might outlive my retirement account.

End of story? Hardly. The questions never stop.

No matter how much comfort and security surrounds me, I still miss my old community of day laborers and migrant workers. I miss the talks among the tree planters, the camaraderie of pickers on the bulb farm, the spontaneous potlucks, and our shared idealism. Those years were less lonely, too. Someone always had a guitar at the ready, an extra pot of lentil soup, and a story of a new place down the road.

This age-old battle to confront and sort from the endless opportunities in this country and to finally hear your own voice emerge, isn't this what creates a life? And as my years drift toward the paunchy and comfortable, I crave my Bohemian past, which revolved around crummy jobs and desperate trips to pawn shops, but which also had a vibrancy and excitement that I miss.

On those long sleepless nights when I try to connect my disparate halves (Did I really live that life? How did I get to be sixty?), I close my eyes and imagine I am once again bouncing up and down in a van to plant America's new forests in the clear-cuts of the Pacific Northwest. I have a silver thermos filled with hot coffee and a paper bag with a cheese sandwich and a blueberry muffin. My boots and socks are dry for the moment but it is raining and will continue to rain all day. The comforting warmth of other men's bodies surrounds me. We cross the long bridge in Astoria from Oregon to Washington. The sun comes up over the Columbia River in pastel shades of pink and blue. The wind blows fierce where river meets the sea. Salmon trawlers and crab boats are already at work, bobbing up and down near the river's wild mouth, their lights reflecting off the water.

In that sweet, holy hour before work I am a young man with a bag of tree plugs. I will climb steep ridges in the grey drizzle. I will dig in the dirt and slash with a thin shovel, and every nine feet I will drop a tree into a hole. I will do this for twelve hours. At the end of the day I will sleep like the dead. For awhile it would be enough.

Standing at the Edge

On the upper deck of the ferry from Seattle to the Olympic Peninsula, a man boldly goes through his T'ai Chi exercises: one leg lifted like a heron hunting for frogs, arms spread out in what looks like a fight stance. Over his right shoulder is Mt. Baker; over his left Mt. Rainier. He maintains perfect balance in the face of strong winds whipping through Puget Sound. Above him is blue sky all the way to Canada with its green cities of Victoria and Vancouver. Across the bow are the distant glacial peaks of the Olympic Mountains.

Here, thirty days from the end of the century, is America: fat, rich, and gleaming, epitomized in the global images of Seattle and Portland, sparkling liberal cities of computer chips, start-up companies, and twenty-year-old millionaires. America now works at home, lounges in bright-colored pajamas, recreates on mountain bikes, and drinks lattes from stainless steel cups guaranteed not to spill. The T'ai Chi dancer circles and twirls so perfectly. On the threshold of the future, he is an elegant link to the past. Seattle fades into the distance, looking like an abandoned Lego set.

Hours after our ferry ride with the T'ai Chi dancer, my wife, Jan, and I hike down the long tongue of land called Dungeness Spit. Cormorants promenade offshore on hidden kelp; camouflaged sandpipers appear and disappear in the sand-colored light as they run the wet border of surf. Scoters dive and rise in a feeding frenzy. Foreign freighters named Faith and Hope with their Pacific Rim booty come down the Strait of Juan de Fuca to and from the Seattle docks. Jan collects ebony stones worn smooth by the waves. I choose egg-white rocks and bleached seal bones. Hand-holding lovers in first bloom pass tired children carried by tired fathers who, in turn, pass middle-aged couples wearing identical sweatshirts emblazoned with the name of Washington's capital Olympia. Forts of driftwood guard the beach. A slice of old-growth spruce trunk with at least three hundred rings sits like a giant disk of stored history.

When I was a child I counted ahead to this point in time, the turn of the century, knew I would be forty-four when it happened, but could not predict what my life would embrace. Now, standing solidly in the year 2000 looking back to the end of last year, I realize I was hungering for a three-dimensional, on-the-ground reality check at the millennium. I craved my own evaluation of our country, separate from the media hype. I wanted to know who America is and what it means to be an American.

To find out, Jan and I had loaded up our tent and sleeping bags and, like our pioneer ancestors, headed west to Washington State's Olympic Peninsula. What I found was both reassuring and unsettling. Even today—two decades later—the details of this road trip remain unsorted. The conclusions may never come.

Probably I failed in my ambitious quest, but I am certain of one thing: To be an American at the turn of the century is to be part of an endless experiment. I came away wanting to immerse myself more deeply in this country's journey, to participate more, to complain less, to revel in our diversity. Maybe I finally found my own definition of patriotism.

On the three-hundred-and-fortieth day of the last year in the twentieth century, I smear on SPF 15 sunscreen without PABA in the parking lot of a McDonald's in Port Townsend, Washington, while Jan washes her hair in the sink of the same restaurant. I have already tidied up with antiseptic soap in the men's room. Another man came in and tried to urinate, but I could tell he was afraid of my appearance: a three-day beard, wrinkled khakis, and dirty pale green shirt. He didn't know I drive a new $22,000 Subaru Forester, that I own nineteen shares of Merrill Lynch stock, and that I just purchased a $35 fleece hat from a man whose business was called "Do Da Productions." I quickly dry my face with abrasive, brown paper towels, and as I open the door to leave I can hear the man finally begin to pee.

At the end of the century, we carry a hundred years of collected fear— scared of those who act out of character, who practice T'ai Chi on ferries, and who take baths in public restrooms.

I am afraid, too. At my last checkup, the doctor gave me a free month's worth of an anti-anxiety pill called "BuSpar." The twenty-one tablets came in a graphically pleasing purple folder with the promise: "Your

PATH to Relief of Persistent Anxiety." Inside the packet are two tiny pamphlets: "What is Anxiety?" and "How BuSpar Can Help." The first pamphlet blames an imbalance of the brain chemical serotonin. But I blame anxiety on millions of dangerous inputs over the years—the Reagan presidency, Three Mile Island, living for too long in paranoid Idaho, being a parent and an ex-husband, a lack of protein in my diet, watching countless episodes of "America's Most Wanted," and banging my head twice on the sharp edge of our garage door.

BuSpar scares me, too. If I take it will I end up like Kesey's Big Chief, an uncreative automaton who laughs at clouds? Is all anxiety necessarily bad? Shouldn't we be moderately afraid of the awesome hand of fate and the fragile nature of our bodies, made of bone and skin? For a year now the drugs have sat unopened in a cardboard box with a dozen small plastic bottles of pilfered motel shampoo. At the century's end, I feel like a rebel for not taking anti-depressants.

In Port Townsend I look over several bonsai trees, including a twisted cypress and a Japanese maple in autumn scarlet. These trees were decades old. I have always wanted a bonsai, in fact, have craved them for twenty-five years. If I had followed up on my interest in 1974, I would have a tree of substance today. How many threads I wish I had pulled! What would my life be like if I had read a poem a day, learned the distinct colors of new bird, written five hundred words, or begun a quilt? But another twenty-four hours of the century are behind us. I don't need any negative thoughts in the night. Night is hard enough.

Tonight I hear the tide swallowing the beach. In the adjoining campsite a woman tries for the high notes in the chorus on Paul Simon's "The Boxer." How rare to hear a live human voice raised in song. Ocean waves eventually drown out the singer and her guitar. No fear at the moment, no room in this rich place for anxiety. The Earth gathers me to her.

With just seventeen days to the closing millennium, I stand in Pacific Beach State Park, at the foot of the tallest Sitka spruce in North America: 270-feet tall, a half a millennium old, twelve-and-a-half feet in diameter, and straight as an arrow. The bark is dimpled like a golf ball. I scrape my hand against the trunk, leaving my DNA. A doe and her fawn stand nearby on a cobbled island in the middle of Hoh River. I look past the giant tree to the devastating scars of industrial logging at the park's entrance. We follow those cuts right down to the Pacific Ocean, where the timber companies ran out of land. Fog is our companion today, and, when we aren't driving through the clear-cuts and burning slash piles, we pass through the monoculture of fast-growing nursery hemlock, some only a few feet tall: new wood in an old-growth world.

Landscape creates moods, and this hammered moonscape brings back my old Northwest depression, even though I left the coast in 1983. Living for years in gray, flat light the color of cigarette smoke will wash you out, will have you sleepy and squinty, not knowing (and, eventually, not caring) what hour of the day it is because the light is the same at 6 p.m. as it is as 8 a.m. BuSpar begins to make sense.

Jan feels the oppression, too, and it takes all my willpower to lead us to a good feeling in which to sleep in an odd, somewhat littered campground, the type of place in which bodies are found. We try to walk off the depression on the clean, perfectly flat beach. There are no rocks anywhere, only the broken change of sand dollars. On the horizon a lone fishing boat bobs and lists in the peaks and valleys of raucous waves.

Down the beach a Best Western stands like a sand castle apparition. After an hour of walking, we drive into the confusing resort town of Ocean Shores, where investors are building hotels and conference centers as the money of this rich decade keeps pouring in. A new intersection has just been built, with McDonald's facing off across the street from Burger King. It's too soon to tell which restaurant will prevail.

We enter an IGA grocery, where we buy raw vegetables, sharp cheese, and caramel corn. We stand behind a teenage mother buying apple juice and formula with her WIC checks. The cashier tries to reassure the mother about parental anxiety. "Oh, that's just part of parenting," the cashier says, smiling in maternal camaraderie.

"Well, that's the part I don't like!" snaps the young mom. I try to avoid guessing her age or her situation, knowing I will sink into an anxious state that can be paralyzing.

We drive back to our campsite somewhat cheered with the promise of hot beans and rice with caramel corn for dessert. The campground is filling up with what I hope are not the men I saw last week on "America's Most Wanted."

In the dark I hear the ocean's surf. Around the campground wet twigs snap in campfires. Somehow, I still feel the need to shake my life up, to sleep outdoors, to see the rain forest, to touch the tallest spruce in America. There really is nothing to fear and everything to cherish.

*

On the final day of 1999, I boil red potatoes and shovel snow from the front sidewalk and driveway. I jog three miles in the fresh snow, check e-mail and stock quotes, and regional newspapers on the Internet. My nineteen-year-old daughter, Rose, calls from her mother's cabin somewhere in the mountains on the Oregon—California border to let me know she arrived safely on Amtrak.

I speak with my neighbor, who, as usual, complains about his job at a local public radio station and wonders out loud how he can retire next year. "I want to go back to teaching music," he says.

My father calls from the east coast of Florida to say the adjustment from Brooklyn to temporary winter living in the sunshine state was easier than he expected. He had his laptop, a phone, and rented furniture.

I take an old, ragged road atlas and cut out all the places I have lived: nine squares and rectangles from the four corners area of the southwest to the north coast of California to the upper peninsula of Michigan. I paste the one of eastern Washington and northern Idaho in my journal with the words: "Here is where I've been living since August 1983." This work makes me sad, maybe because time passes so quickly, or simply because I am nostalgic for mountains, oceans, and deserts all at the same time.

Jan bakes rosemary potatoes in the oven and I poach eggs to break on top of the potatoes. We have no real plans. We haven't bought into the drama of Y2K, and although I did fill up the Subaru with gas, we didn't purchase extra water, batteries, or peanut butter. Instead of waiting for mishaps we make the sweetest love imaginable, while our smallest tabby cat Toby watches.

CSPAN airs a live broadcast of President Clinton, Hillary, and Chelsea receiving 360 guests at the White House Millennium Dinner, an event to honor creativity. I see Sophia Loren, staying close to the President during the dinner toast, basketball legend Bill Russell, Martin Scorcese, Jack Nicholson, and many bejeweled people I don't recognize. After the toast, the White House closes the party to CSPAN, and a Washington Post "style" reporter comes on to complain about the closure. She wears an evening gown and is whiny.

I follow New Year's in Paris, London, Barcelona, Iceland, Easter Island, Brazil, Fiji, Egypt, and Amsterdam, where two men open the new century with an open-mouthed kiss. Times Square has perhaps two million happy, healthy, brave, rich partygoers secured behind fenced "pens." Police pace in front nervously, but they notice nothing out of the ordinary, not even the mammoth advertisement for Discover Card just below the 2000 sign in the square.

As the new year falls across Tucson, a huge Native American round dance takes place, where a thousand people of many hues and backgrounds sweetly shuffle together in a circle. Peace reigns across the planet despite our worst predictions concerning our worst motives. And when the clock strikes midnight here in the little wheat town of Pullman, Washington, fireworks splatter into the air over Main Street, and our neighbor steps outside to shoot off six rounds from a handgun. I instinctively duck, then creep into the bedroom to kiss Jan and tell her I love her as much (if not more) in the new century as in the old.

On the first day of 2000, everything feels different, and in my mind's eye I see a blank slate, a new start, and a delicious opportunity like no other I've been granted. All the mistakes of the last one hundred years and beyond are history, as are the ones I personally contributed to our collective mess. Still, I can't help but feel optimistic as I step cautiously outside into the new year. I have not told a lie yet. Neither have I said a negative word about anyone. Nor have I betrayed a single soul. The chance to be humble, kind, and helpful beckons like a golden path.

From my tiny place on this beautiful planet, I look up at the heavens. Stars and planets shine brightly off in the eastern horizon: the Pleiades, Mars, and the Big Dipper. Great-horned owls call to each other, and coyotes bark and howl nearby. And down toward town, the most beautiful sound of all: the irrepressible sound of human laughter.

Stephen J. Lyons is the author of four books of essays and journalism: *Landscape of the Heart: Writings on Daughters and Journeys, A View from the Inland Northwest, The 1,000-Year Flood: Destruction, Loss, Rescue, and Redemption along the Mississippi River,* and *Going Driftless: Life Lessons from the Heartland for Unraveling Times.*

Stephen is a two-time recipient of a fellowship in prose writing from the Illinois Arts Council and has published articles, reviews, essays, and poems in numerous publications, including *Wall Street Journal, Washington Post, Salon, The Independent, Toronto Globe & Mail, Manoa, Newsweek, The Sun, Chicago Tribune, Funny Times, Witness,* and *High Country News.* His work has been featured in fourteen anthologies alongside such noted writers as Barry Lopez, Peter Matthiessen, Edward Abbey, Barbara Kingsolver, Anna Quindlen, Dave Barry, and Louise Erdrich. Stephen's books include blurbs by Terry Tempest Williams, William Kittredge, and Bill McKibben.

Stephen is a native of the South Side of Chicago and a product of that city's legendary public education system. After living for thirty years in the West, he now resides in a small farming town in central Illinois that often smells of soy. He's been employed in nine different states as a tree planter, daffodil picker, dude ranch cook, a model for Porsche, ice cream vendor, magazine editor, phone solicitor, newspaper reporter, tofu maker, grain truck driver, assistant dairy herdsman, and agricultural extension editor. He once worked for a week in Colorado pulling nails out of two-by-fours, and for one twelve-hour day picking hops in southern Oregon until he was fired for claiming the foreman had bad karma.